Quilling
Australian
Native Flowers

Quilling Australian Native Flowers

15 NEW DESIGNS

Jean Woolston-Hamey

Kangaroo Press

*Dedicated to my aunt, Elsie Hamey,
who took the time to introduce me
to quilling—thank you*

Acknowledgments
Thanks to the following businesses in
Coffs Harbour for their assistance:
  Carousel Art and Craft Supplies
  Coffs Office Supplies
  Park Beach Plaza Newsagents
  Coffs City Printing

Thanks also to Leonard Cronin for the book
The Concise Australian Flora, which I used as a
guide for many of my patterns, and to Sylvia
DeNeiderhausen for her encouragement.

Photography by Bob Weeks Photography,
Coffs Harbour

*First published in 1995 by Kangaroo Press Pty Ltd
3 Whitehall Road Kenthurst NSW 2156 Australia
PO Box 6125 Dural Delivery Centre NSW 2158
Printed in Hong Kong through Colorcraft Ltd*

ISBN 0 86417 724 0

Contents

Introduction

My long-term love affair with Australian native flowers, combined with my discovery of quilling, has inspired this collection of flower portraits. I found that quilling provided the perfect medium to create something beautifully Australian.

If you find quilling as interesting as I do, you will find many uses for these patterns. Use them complete on wall plaques, in frames or on plates, or use single stems or just the blossoms to decorate gift cards or place-names. Whichever way you use them, I hope you enjoy the challenge.

One of the great things about quilling flowers like these is that you do not have to be as precise as with standard quilling. Just as each flower and leaf in nature is a little different, so their quilled representations do not have to be exactly the same. A lot of the flowers I have chosen have more than one colour form, so you could end up creating a rainbow.

I hope this book will help to expand your appreciation of the wonderful diversity of Australia's native plant life.

Materials and equipment

Each quilling pattern is set on a background measuring 21 cm × 25 cm (8¼" × 9¾").

Although I cut all my quilling papers myself I have tried to keep most of the measurements the same as the pre-cut quilling papers that can be bought from craft shops. Equivalent Imperial measurements are included in each section.

I have used two types of paper: Mois Optix 80 gsm photocopy paper, available from office supply shops in A4 sheets, for most of the blossoms, and Canson Mi-Teintes art paper, available in 160 gsm sheets from good art supply shops. I have given the colour names and/or numbers and a colour that can be substituted if the others are not available.

The tools used are very simple and easy to obtain:
- needle-type quilling tool (no other quilling tool is needed)
- stitch ripper (found in many a sewing box); the back of the blade is used for all embossing
- small sharp scissors
- pointed tweezers
- toothpicks or satay sticks (for applying glue)
- Blu-Tack (to hold pieces in position while glue is drying)
- craft knife
- soft pencil sharpened to a fine point
- soft eraser for removing pencil lines and for curling petals on
- white paste (Perkins Paste or similar)
- white craft glue, clear-drying
- cardboard or heavy paper for cutting leaf and petal patterns
- steel ruler showing both centimetres and millimetres
- fringing tool (not essential, but very handy; scissors will be fine)
- hole punch
- Scribblers (dimensional paint)
- small flat paintbrush (for applying dimensional paint)
- no. 10 knitting needle for making paper tube
- meat skewer with rounded end, or something similar

Basic instructions

The basic quilling shapes used include the tight coil, the loose coil (pressed into a star shape), the cone and the cup or bell shape. Cup, bell and cone shapes can be made from a tight coil with the end glued and the centre gently pushed outwards to the desired shape. Some of these shapes will have pointed ends while some are blunt or flat. When the coil has been formed to the required shape, spread glue on the inside so the cup, bell or cone will hold its shape, and allow to dry before use.

I have included an actual-size stem chart with each pattern as the stems in the finished pieces are often hidden by the leaves and blossoms. On all patterns the stems are attached first.

In nearly all cases the blossoms are attached to the stems first, then the leaves. The pattern instructions clearly specify where this order is reversed.

Actual size leaf and petal patterns are given for each flower. You will have to trace these onto cardboard to make templates to keep leaf and petal sizes even.

Where two different-coloured papers must be glued together, as for the boronia petals (page 40), use white paste rather than hobby glue, which can cause the paper to wrinkle.

The dimensional paint used in this book comes from the Scribblers range. The colours used, and how it is to be applied, are noted on each pattern. Different brands of dimensional paint can be used as long as the colours are similar.

If you are building the patterns onto plastic or glass, or any surface other than cardboard or paper, you will need to use a stronger glue than Perkins Paste or craft glue to attach the pieces.

I hope you enjoy quilling your Australian natives as much as I do.

Peach-blossom tea tree

Leptospermum squarrosum

Illustrated on page 18

A stiff bushy shrub to 3 metres. The flowers, either pink or white, appear along the stems and branches during spring and summer, creating a spectacular display. After flowering, small woody cup-shaped seed capsules appear. The plant is good for gardens and parks in sandy soil on the coast and tablelands of New South Wales.

The word *squarrosum* refers to the roughness of the bark.

Papers

Blossoms   Optic Tula Pink (pale pink) for petals
    Canson 480 Vert amande (pale green) for cups
Leaves   Canson Vert amande (pale green)
Stems   Canson Vert pomme (medium green)

Construction

Blossoms

Using a hole-punch and the pink paper, punch out 180 complete discs.

Cut 90 strips 1.5 mm × 1.5 cm in pink.

Glue a disc to each end of the strips, making sure the strip reaches across the full width of the disc (this is for strength). Each glued strip should look like this:

Cut across each strip in the centre, creating 2 petals with stems.

Cut 36 strips 5 mm × 2 cm in pink, and fringe them.
Cut 36 strips 2 mm × 9 cm in light green.
Cut 36 strips 2 mm × 3 cm in light green.

Make 36 long strips, joining the short strips in this order, and overlapping the ends 2 mm:
    9 cm light green strip
    + 2 cm fringed pink strip
    + 3 cm light green strip

On the 3 cm light green strip, starting 1 cm away from the pink fringed strip, attach 5 petals *by their stems* at 3 mm intervals, *overlapping* the petal

discs. When all parts are dry start coiling from the 9 cm light green end, forming a cup shape until you reach the fringed strip. Coil straight from this point so the fringing and petals are level.

Apply glue to the full length of the 3 cm light green section with petals. This will help hold the top section firmly in place when adjusting petals. Allow to dry thoroughly. Now spread petals outward away from fringing and gently ease each petal to form an even circle around the centre.

Leaves

Cut 95 leaves from the pattern in pale green.

Emboss a mid-rib from tip to base.

Stems

In medium green, cut:
1 strip 3 mm × 19.5 cm
1 strip 3 mm × 18 cm
1 strip 3 mm × 15 cm
4 strips 3 mm × 7 cm
1 strip 3 mm × 6 cm
1 strip 3 mm × 5 cm
2 strips 3 mm × 4 cm
1 strip 3 mm × 3 cm
1 strip 3 mm × 2.5 cm

Approx: 1.5 mm = ¹⁄₁₆"; 2 mm = ³⁄₃₂"; 3 mm = ¹⁄₈"; 5 mm = ¼"; 1.5 cm = ½"; 2 cm = ¾"; 2.5 cm = 1"; 3 cm = 1¼"; 4 cm = 1½"; 5 cm = 2"; 6 cm = 2¼"; 7 cm = 2¾"; 15 cm = 5¾"; 18 cm = 7"; 19.5 cm = 7½"

Mounting

1. Position and glue stems following stem chart.
2. Position leaves in groups of 2 or 3 at the tips of each stem.
3. Position the rest of the leaves at 3–4 cm spacing in an alternating pattern down all stems until all leaves are used.
4. Position 1 blossom at the tip of each stem between leaves.

5. Position the rest of the blossoms down each stem at points opposite each leaf. Attach some flat and others at angles that please you. Keep the blossoms mostly to the tops and middles of the stems; the bottom sections should be just leaves.

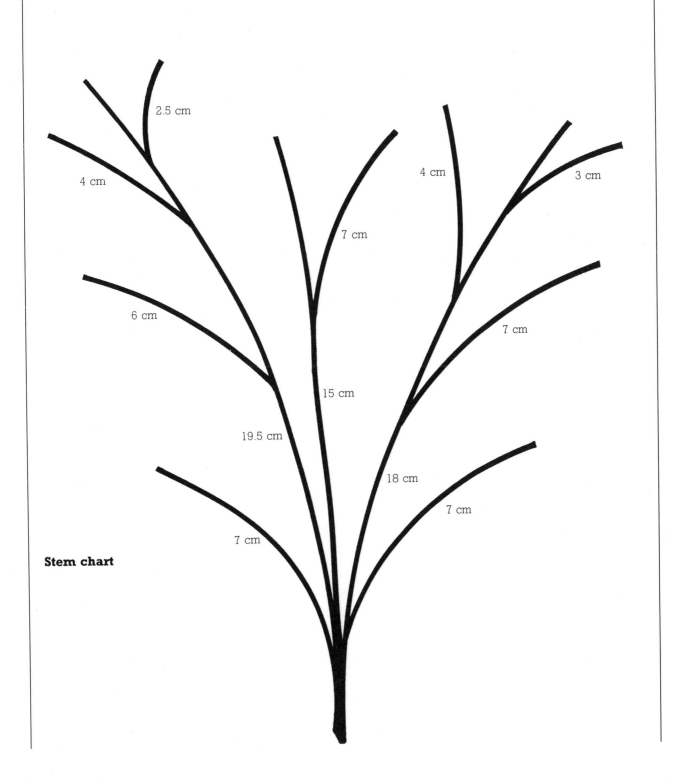

Stem chart

Red morrell

Eucalyptus longicornis

Illustrated on page 24

An upright small to medium tree to about 20 metres with a cylindrical trunk covered with rough, fibrous grey bark which also occurs on the lower branches. The upper branches are reddish in colour, hence the name red morrell, as are the flower buds that open into white or cream flowers. The flowers are arranged in a wagon wheel or half wheel shape, and open in the late spring and into summer. This tree enjoys the sandy or loamy soils around the goldfields of south-west Western Australia.

The word *longicornis* refers to the horned shape of the bud.

Papers

Blossoms Optic Zoda Lemon (light lemon yellow) for petals
Canson 475 Vert pomme (medium green) for cups
Optic Koda Caramel (light apricot) for centres and buds
Leaves Canson 475 Vert pomme (medium green)
Stems Canson 340 Chanvre clair (light grey-brown)

Construction

Blossoms
Cut 69 strips 1 cm × 8 cm in lemon, and fringe them.
Cut 69 strips 2 mm × 8.5 cm in light apricot.

Join 1 lemon fringed strip to the end of 1 plain apricot strip. Coil from apricot end (do not cup), keeping coil firm when glueing.

Cups Cut 69 strips 2 mm × 14 cm in medium green.
Coil to cup shape (see sketch) and glue.

When blossoms and cups are dry, glue the solid end of the blossom into the open end of the cup and allow to dry, then spread the fringing outwards to expose the apricot centre.

Glue 5 groups of 5 blossoms in an even wheel shape with the cup tips all touching. Glue 11 groups of 4 in half wheels with all cup tips touching. *Allow all wheels to dry thoroughly.*

Unopened buds Cut 14 strips 2 mm × 15 cm in apricot. Coil each strip into a long cone (see sketch).

Bud cups Cut 14 strips 2 mm × 14 cm in medium green. Coil and glue the same as for open blossoms.

When buds and cups are dry, glue open ends together.

Glue 2 groups of 5 buds into a wheel shape with cup tips touching. Glue 1 half wheel of 4. Allow all wheels to dry thoroughly.

Leaves
Cut 14 leaves from pattern 1 in medium green.
Cut 5 leaves from pattern 2 in medium green.

Emboss mid-rib from tip to base.

1   2

Stems

In light grey-brown, cut:

   1 strip 3 mm × 20 cm
   2 strips 3 mm × 8 cm
   1 strip 3 mm × 7 cm
   1 strip 3 mm × 6.5 cm
   1 strip 3 mm × 6 cm
   1 strip 3 mm × 5 cm
   11 strips 3 mm × 1.5 cm

Approx: 1.5 mm = ¹/₁₆"; 2 mm = ³/₃₂"; 3 mm = ⅛"; 1 cm = ⅜"; 1.5 cm = ½"; 5 cm = 2"; 6 cm = 2¼"; 6.5 cm = 2½"; 7 cm = 2¾"; 8 cm = 3"; 8.5 cm = 3¼"; 14 cm = 5½"; 20 cm = 8"

Mounting

1. Position and glue stems following stem chart.
2. Position blossom wheels and half wheels at the ends of each stem. Following the photograph, lay all full wheels flat and half wheels either upright or at an angle. The 4-bud half wheel can sit halfway down the stem of a full wheel bud stem.
3. Position all leaves at a stem axis, either singly or in twos. Not every stem axis needs a leaf so you can position them as you like, remembering that the smaller leaves should be at the tops of the stems.

Stem chart

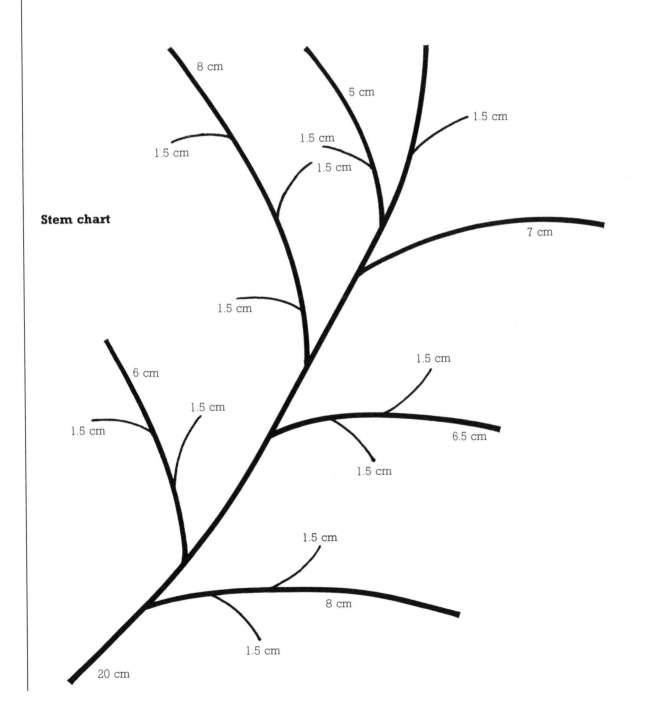

Native bluebell

Sollya heterophylla

Illustrated on page 25

A quick-growing woody, twining or bushy small shrub, becoming popular with home gardeners. The dainty bell-like flowers come in light or dark blue, white, and sometimes pink. They form loose pendulous clusters which open in the spring and summer and are followed by almost black, small sausage-like seed pods. This little native grows naturally in sandy or gravelly soils along the Western Australian coast.

Sollya—named after botanist R. H. Solly 1778–1858.
The word *heterophylla* means 'variable leaves'.

Papers

Blossoms Optic Visa Blue (pale blue) for petals
   Optic Zoda Lemon (lemon yellow) for stigma
Buds Optic Visa Blue (pale blue)
Leaves Canson Vert amande (pale green) for new growth
   Canson Vert pomme (mid green) for older leaves
Stems Canson 132 Liege (light brown)
   Canson 352 Rose fonce (orange pink) for flower stems

Construction

Blossoms

Cut 1 sheet 14 cm × 15 cm in pale blue. From this sheet cut 95 petals following the pattern (5 petals per blossom). Fold petals along score line.

Cups Cut 19 strips 2 mm × 19 cm in pale blue. Coil to cup shape and glue.

Stigma Cut 19 strips 2 mm × 10 cm in lemon yellow. Coil to a long cone shape and glue inside to hold shape. Allow to dry, then glue open end inside the open end of the blue cup.

Glue the wide end of each petal to the outside edge of the widest coil of the blue cup, so the petals cover the yellow centre, overlapping the petals slightly. Allow each petal to dry before attaching the next one. When all 5 petals are attached and dry, gently ease petals outwards for a more open bloom.

Buds Cut 4 strips 2 mm × 19 cm in pale blue and coil to cone shapes, glueing inside cone to keep shape.

Cut 4 strips 2 mm × 15 cm in pale blue and coil to cup shape.

Glue the open ends of the cones and cups together and allow to dry thoroughly.

Leaves

Cut a piece of pale green paper 17 cm × 4 cm, coat with white glue and allow to dry. From it cut 16 leaves from pattern 1, shiny side up.

Cut a piece of mid green paper 20 cm × 6 cm, coat with white glue and allow to dry. From it cut 13 leaves from pattern 2, shiny side up.

Emboss mid-rib from base to tip on all leaves.

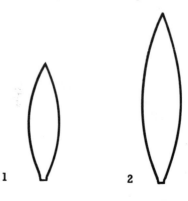

1   2

Stems

Flower stems From orange pink paper cut:

7 strips 2 mm × 1 cm

9 strips 2 mm × 1.5 cm

4 strips 2 mm × 2 cm

2 strips 2 mm × 2.5 cm

8 strips 2 mm × 3 cm (these 8 strips are attached to the main stems, and the other flower stems are attached to these, following the stem pattern)

Mounting

1. Position and glue stems following stem chart.

2. Attach the eight 3 cm strips for the flower heads along the broken lines.

3. Attach the smaller flower head strips in groups of 2 or 3, varying the lengths in each group.

4. Attach single blossoms and buds to the ends of the flower head stalks. One stalk only carries 2 buds.

5. Attach pale green leaves glossy side up, in groups of 2 or 3, to the tips of all main stems, with 1 or 2 leaves alternating 1 cm down from the tip on the two main stems.

6. Attach mid green leaves glossy side up in alternating pattern at 3–4 cm spacings until all leaves are used up.

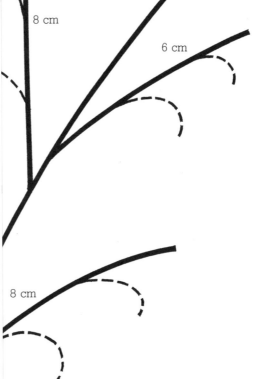

Approx: 2 mm = ³⁄₃₂"; 1 cm = ³⁄₈"; 1.5 cm = ¹⁄₂"; 2 cm = ³⁄₄"; 3 cm = 1¹⁄₄"; 6 cm = 2¹⁄₄"; 8 cm = 3"; 10 cm = 4"; 14 cm = 5¹⁄₂"; 15 cm = 5³⁄₄"; 17 cm = 6¹⁄₂"; 18 cm = 7"; 19 cm = 7¹⁄₂"; 20 cm = 8"

Marri

Eucalyptus calophylla

A thick trunked, medium to tall tree to about 40 metres with a dense crown. The bark is grey and darkens with age. The leaves are smaller than in most eucalypts and have a glossy sheen. The pink or white flowers emerge in clusters during late summer and autumn. This tree is often grown for its attractive flowers which can be easily seen above the leaves. It prefers sandy soils in open forests in coastal or mountain areas of Western Australia, and is becoming popular in the eastern states.

The word *calophylla* means 'beautiful leaves'.

Papers

Blossoms Optic Vero Pink (dark pink)
  Optic Vada Blonde (creamy yellow) for centres and stigmas
Buds Canson 480 Vert amande (pale green)
Growth tips Canson 480 Vert amande (pale green)
Seed cups Canson 501 Marron fonce (tobacco brown)
Leaves Canson 475 Vert pomme (medium green)
Stems Canson 501 Marron fonce (tobacco brown)
and Scribblers dimensional paints, SC224 Iridescent Gold and SC136 Shiny Chiffon Green

Construction

Blossoms
From the dark pink paper cut 21 strips 1 cm × 7 cm and fringe them finely.

Centre Cut 21 straight strips 3 mm × 6 cm in cream.

Stigma Cut 21 long thin tapered strips 1 cm long in cream.

Join one of each piece with the stigma at right angles on one end of the straight cream strip and the fringed strip on the other end (see sketch).

Coil from the stigma end. Spread the fringing to expose the cream centre. Brush tips of fringing with Iridescent Gold Scribblers paint, and coat the very tip of the stigma with Shiny Chiffon Green.

Buds
From the pale green paper, cut 8 strips 2 mm × 19 cm.

Coil 4 strips into a wide cup shape:

Coil 4 strips into a long cup shape:

Glue one of each cup together at open ends.

Growth tips
From the pale green paper, cut 4 strips 3 mm × 5.5 cm.

Coil them into small cone shapes and glue. When dry flatten sideways.

Seed cups
From the tobacco brown paper, cut 7 strips 2 mm × 10 cm, and coil to open cup shapes similar to the bud cup.

Marri

Peach-blossom tea tree *(instructions page 10)*

Leaves

From mid green paper, cut a piece 36 cm × 9 cm. Coat the paper on one side with white glue and allow to dry. The glue will make the paper glossy. Cut all leaves from the same side of this piece.

Cut 17 leaves from the leaf pattern, then turn the pattern over and cut another 17 leaves. This will give half the leaves a right curve and half the leaves a left curve. Emboss mid-rib from base to tip.

Stems

From tobacco brown paper, cut:
 1 strip 3 mm × 11.5 cm
 1 strip 3 mm × 11 cm
 1 strip 3 mm × 9 cm
 1 strip 3 mm × 8 cm
 1 strip 3 mm × 7 cm

(continued on next page)

Stem chart

*1 strip 3 mm × 6 cm

*1 strip 3 mm × 8.5 cm (bend back the first 5 mm and glue down)

*1 strip 3 mm × 6 cm (bend back the first 5 mm and glue down)

Take the three strips marked * and join them together thus: glue the doubled end of the 8.5 cm strip to the *single-thickness* end of the 6 cm strip with the doubled end, then join the doubled end of this strip to the plain 6 cm strip. Make sure the joints overlap, making a ridge, and that both joints are on the same side of the strip (see stem chart). This is the main stem.

Approx: 3 mm = ⅛"; 5 mm = ¼"; 1 cm = ⅜"; 5.5 cm = 2⅛"; 6 cm = 2¼"; 7 cm = 2¾"; 8 cm = 3"; 8.5 cm = 3¼"; 9 cm = 3½"; 10 cm = 4"; 11 cm = 4¼"; 11.5 cm = 4⅜"; 36 cm = 14"

Mounting

1. Position and glue stems following stem chart.
2. Position growth tips on the very ends of 4 stems. The one stem without a growth tip will be the seed cup stem. Do not use the main stem for the seed cup stem.
3. Position blossoms in groups of 3 and one group of 4, using the photograph as a guide. One of the groups of 3 will have a bud as well.
4. Make one group of 2 flowers with 3 buds.
5. Attach seed cups in 2 groups, one of 4 and one of 3, about 2 cm apart.
6. Attach leaves shiny side up, in pairs or singly spaced, at about 2 cm intervals down the stems. The leaves should point downwards along the stems except for those at the very tips of the stems, which can point upwards or sideways.

Crimson bottlebrush

Callistemon citrinus

Illustrated on page 23

A rather tangled stiff large shrub, growing to about 8 metres. The flowers really do look like bottlebrushes. They are either white or most commonly brilliant red, and are also available in a variety of natural hybrids. Native birds enjoy feeding on these showy blossoms when they open in the spring and summer. A damp swampy area or river bank suits this shrub very nicely and it is common along the coast of eastern Australia. In full bloom it makes a striking display.

The word *citrinus* means 'lemon-like'.

Papers

Blossoms   Optic Raza Red (bright red)
   Optic Reva Green (green)
Seed cups   Canson 475 Vert pomme (mid green)
Leaves   Canson 475 Vert pomme (mid green) for large leaves
   Canson 480 Vert amande (pale green) for small leaves
Stems   Canson 132 Leige (mid brown)
and Scribblers SC224 Iridescent Gold dimensional paint

Construction

Blossoms
In red cut 34 strips 1 cm × 6 cm and fringe them very finely.

In green cut 34 strips 1.5 mm × 10 cm. *Break* each green strip at 8 cm so you have two pieces 8 cm and 2 cm long.

For the stigma cut 34 long thin strips in red, each 1.5 cm long. Join one of each of the blossom pieces in a long strip following the drawing below.

Coil from stigma end and glue. When dry spread the fringing outwards.

Seed cups
From the mid green paper, cut 6 strips 1.5 mm × 8.5 cm. Coil to an open cup shape and glue:

In mid green cut 6 strips 1 mm × 4.5 cm. Make into flat coils and glue inside cups.

Leaves
Cut 19 leaves from pattern 1 in pale green paper.
Cut 10 leaves from pattern 2 in mid green paper.
Cut 10 leaves from pattern 3 in mid green paper.
Emboss each leaf with a mid-rib from tip to base.

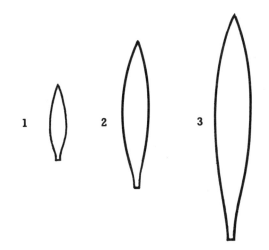

Stems
From mid brown paper, cut:
   1 strip 2 mm × 15 cm
   2 strips 2 mm × 12 cm
   1 strip 2 mm × 7 cm

Approx: 1 mm = $^3/_{64}$"; 1.5 mm = $^1/_{16}$"; 2 mm = $^3/_{32}$"; 1.5 cm = $^1/_2$"; 2 cm = $^3/_4$"; 4.5 cm = $1^3/_4$"; 6 cm = $2^1/_4$"; 7 cm = $2^3/_4$"; 8 cm = 3"; 8.5 cm = $3^1/_4$"; 10 cm = 4"; 12 cm = 5"; 15 cm = $5^3/_4$"

stigma   fringed red

8 cm green   2 cm green

Mounting

1. Position stems following stem chart.
2. Glue small leaves at the very tip of each stem in one group of 3 and three groups of 4. Keep the last 4 small leaves to be attached below the finished central flower brush.
3. Starting 5 mm down from the tip of the stem, attach blossoms in 3 parallel rows. Glue 5 blossoms down one side of the stem and 5 down the other side; glue the third row, of 6 blossoms, along the top edge between the first two rows. Allow each row to dry before adding the next row.
4. Make the second brush the same way.
5. For the small brush start 1 cm down from the small leaves, placing two blossoms opposite each other on either side of stem and two on the edge of the stem as in the photograph.
6. Attach the last 4 small leaves 1 cm below the bottom blossom of the centre brush, with the tips of the leaves touching the fringing of the bottom blossoms.
7. Attach seed cups in random order just below the 4 small leaves on the centre stem.
8. Attach 6 of the medium size leaves in an alternating pattern down the stem without flowers; add 2 medium leaves just below the side brush and the small brush.
9. Attach the 10 largest leaves in an alternating pattern down the rest of the stems, following the photograph.
10. To finish off, brush the tips of the flower fringing with Iridescent Gold dimensional paint.

Stem chart

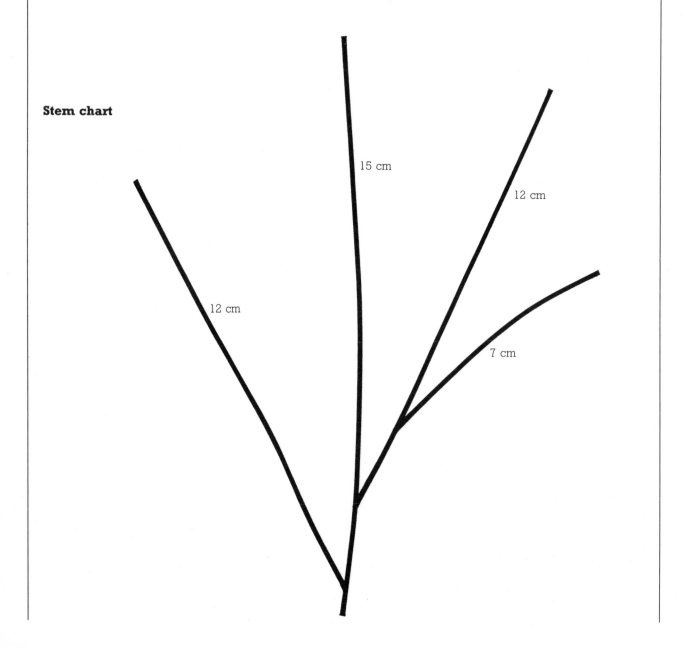

Crimson bottlebrush (instructions page 21)

Red morell *(instructions page 12)*

Native bluebell *(instructions page 14)*

Golden everlasting daisy

Golden everlasting daisy

Helichrysum bracteatum

A stiff annual herb that grows to about 1 metre high. The bright yellow glossy flowers have a papery feel and are often used in dried flower arrangements, as they keep their colour and shape for a long time. Everlastings flower in winter and spring and grow wild along beach areas, in open forests and even in farm paddocks in most areas of Australia.

The word *helichrysum* means 'sun gold'.

Papers

Blossoms Optic Tera Yellow (bright yellow) for the petals
  Canson Vert amande (pale green) for the cup base
Leaves Canson Vert pomme (medium green) for new leaves
  Canson Vert amande (pale green) for old leaves
Stems Canson Vert amande (pale green)

Construction

Blossoms

From the yellow paper, for the centres, cut:
  7 strips 2 mm × 26 cm
  7 strips 4 mm × 26 cm

Fringe the 4 mm strips. Join 1 plain and 1 fringed strip together to make 7 long strips. Coil from the plain end, making a flat disc with fringing on the outside.

For the petals, cut a piece of yellow paper 8 cm × 25 cm, coat with white glue and allow to dry.

Cut 11 petals from pattern 1 for each blossom.
Cut 22 petals from pattern 2 for each blossom.

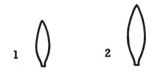

Using a round-ended blunt instrument (I use the handle of a stitch ripper) and a soft eraser, place each petal on the eraser, glued surface uppermost, and press down and along the petal with the handle of the stitch ripper to make the petal curl upwards.

To attach the petals to the central coil, bend the square end of each petal (glossy side up) down at 90°. Attach one petal at a time to the side of the coil below the fringing. Use the smaller petals for the first row. Attach the first row of larger petals in the spaces between the petals of the first row, and the second row of larger petals between those petals. When all petals have dried, attach the cup base.

Cup bases From the pale green paper, cut 4 strips 1.5 mm × 56 cm. Coil them to a deep wide cup shape to fit over the centre base of 4 of the flowers. The other blossoms will be attached flat.

Bud

From the yellow paper, cut:
  1 strip 1.5 mm × 52 cm
  1 strip 1.5 mm × 41 cm

Coil each strip into a cup shape, then glue the open end of the smaller cup inside the open end of the larger one. Dry.

Bud petals Cut 12 yellow petals from pattern 1, but do not curve them. Attach 5 petals around the widest point of the larger cup to cover part of the smaller cup, and attach the other 7 petals 5 mm down from the first row.

Stem chart

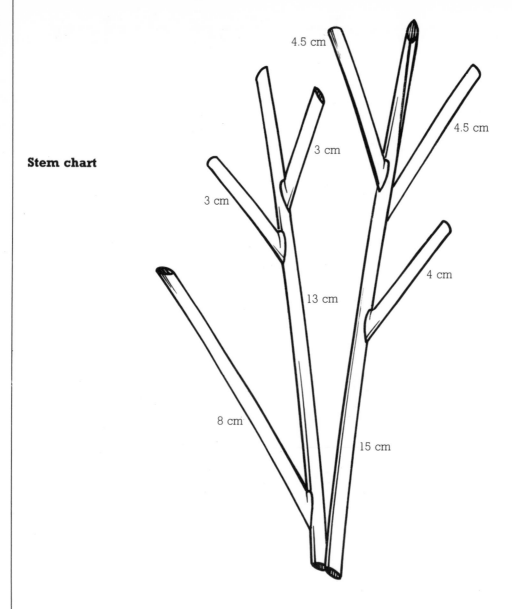

4.5 cm

4.5 cm

3 cm

3 cm

4 cm

13 cm

8 cm

15 cm

Bud cup Cut 1 light green strip 1.5 mm × 33 cm. Coil to a cup shape to fit over the base of the bud and cover the bases of the second row of petals. Glue and allow to dry.

Leaves

From the medium green paper, cut:
    2 leaves from pattern 1
    5 leaves from pattern 2
    6 leaves from pattern 3

From the pale green paper, cut 2 leaves from pattern 3.

Emboss all leaves as shown on the patterns.

Gently fold all smaller leaves lengthwise and twist slightly; unfold them but do not straighten out.

The 2 pale green leaves should be twisted lengthwise to look a bit withered and old, as in the photograph.

Stems

From the pale green paper, cut:
    1 strip 1.5 cm × 15 cm
    1 strip 1.5 cm × 13 cm
    1 strip 1.5 cm × 10 cm
    1 strip 1.5 cm × 9 cm
    1 strip 1.5 cm × 8 cm

Roll each strip into a long roll around a knitting needle (or something similar), glue and allow to dry.

● Trim one end of the 8 cm roll at about 35°

- Cut the 9 cm roll into two 4.5 cm lengths trimmed to 35° at one end.
- Cut the 10 cm roll into two 3 cm lengths and a 4 cm length, each trimmed at 35° at one end.

Approx: 1.5 mm = $^1/_{16}$"; 2 mm = $^3/_{32}$"; 4 mm = $^3/_{16}$"; 5 mm = $^1/_4$"; 3 cm = $1^1/_4$"; 4.5 cm = $1^3/_4$"; 8 cm = 3"; 9 cm = $3^1/_2$"; 10 cm = 4"; 13 cm = $5^1/_4$"; 15 cm = $5^3/_4$"; 26 cm = $10^1/_4$"; 33 cm = 13"; 41 cm = 16"; 52 cm = $20^1/_2$"

Mounting

1. Attach stem rolls following the stem chart, with the angled ends against the main stems.

2. Attach the 3 uncupped blossoms flat at the tops of 3 stems.

3. Attach the cupped blossoms on the other stem tops at an angle to expose the cups. You may need to ease some of the petals into a semi-closed position to make a pleasing arrangement—see the photograph.

4. Attach the bud at the top of the smallest stem so it lines up with it.

5. Attach smaller leaves to the upper sections of the stems, making sure they hug the stem joints.

6. Attach all larger medium green leaves to the very base of the main stem. Glue them in a fan shape covering part of the stems.

7. Attach the 2 pale green old leaves last, parallel with the ground.

Ovens everlasting daisy

Ozothamnus (formerly *Helichrysum*) *stirlingii*

Most Australians are unaware of this unusual sub-alpine daisy as it grows only in the colder regions (above 1000 metres) of the Snowy Mountains in southern New South Wales–northern Victoria and flowers in the summer. It grows to around 3 metres and is rather open in its habit with aromatic leaves. The flowers are button-like, papery in texture and grow in loose clusters. Their large brown centres are surrounded by small blunt white petals.

Ozo refers to smell, and *thamnus* refers to leaves.

Papers

Blossoms Canson 501 Marron fonce (dark brown) for the centres
Optic White (plain white) for the petals
Leaves Canson 480 Vert amande (pale green) for the upper surface
Optic Vada Blonde (cream) for the under surface
Stems Optic Vada Blonde (cream) in double and quadruple thicknesses

Construction

Blossoms
For the centres, from dark brown paper, cut:
11 strips 5 mm × 33 cm
6 strips 5 mm × 25 cm

Make a shallow fringe on each strip before coiling it firmly with a domed centre. Coat inside with glue to hold in place and allow to dry thoroughly.

Petals Cut 186 petals in white paper from pattern:

Use 12 petals on each of the large centres, and 9 petals on the smaller centres.

Bend 2 mm of the narrow end of each petal down at right angles and attach it to the side of the centre below fringing. Attach one petal at a time, bending it out from the centre, with the widest part of the petal just touching the next one. Continue right around centre in this manner. Allow to dry thoroughly.

Cup base Cut 7 strips 1.5 mm × 27 cm in pale green. Coil to a deep cup shape to fit over the base of the brown centres, glue to hold shape and dry before attaching. The other 10 flowers are attached flat.

Leaves
Cut 1 strip 3 cm × 24 cm in both pale green and cream, glue together and allow to dry flat under slight pressure, then cut 3 leaves from pattern 1.

Cut 1 strip 2.5 cm × 18 cm in both pale green and cream, glue together and allow to dry flat under slight pressure, then cut 3 leaves from pattern 2.

Emboss all leaves on the green side with mid-rib and side veins following the patterns. Fold the leaves lengthwise along mid-rib so they don't sit flat when attached to stems.

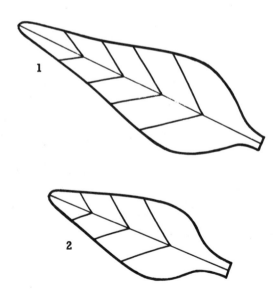

Ovens everlasting daisy

Violet kunzea *(instructions page 36)*

Flax wattle *(instructions page 38)*

Mottlecah *(instructions page 49)*

Stems

Main stems In cream paper, cut:

    4 strips 3 mm × 12 cm and glue all 4 together flat

    4 strips 3 mm × 10.5 cm and glue all 4 together flat

    4 strips 3 mm × 6 cm and glue all 4 together flat

Blossom stems In cream paper, cut 28 strips 3 mm × 1.5 cm and glue together in pairs.

Approx: 3 mm = ⅛"; 5 mm = ¼"; 1.5 cm = ½"; 6 cm = 2¼"; 10.5 cm = 4¼"; 12 cm = 5"; 18 cm = 7"; 24 cm = 9½"; 25 cm = 9¾"; 27 cm = 10½"; 33 cm = 13"

Mounting

1. Position and glue stems following stem chart.
2. Position 1 blossom at the end of each small stem. The cupped blossoms are attached at an angle while the uncupped blossoms are attached flat.
3. Attach the smaller leaves first, with 2 alternately on the long stem and 1 on the short stem.
4. Attach 2 large leaves at the very base of the stem and the last large leaf at the point where the main stems join.

Stem chart

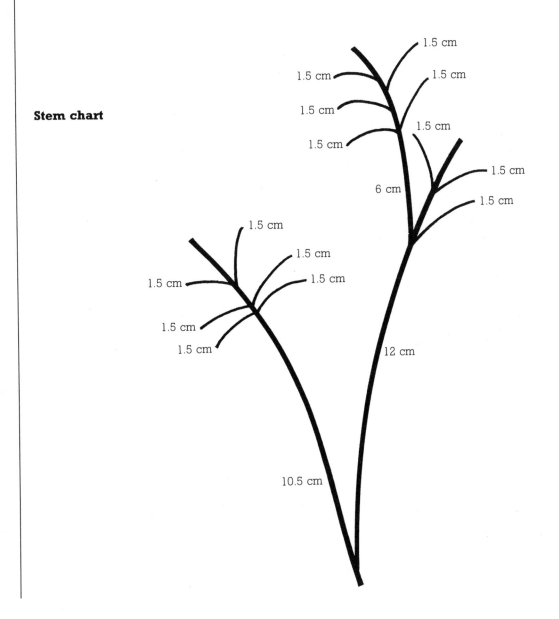

Violet kunzea

Kunzea parvifolia

Illustrated on page 32

One of my favourite shrubs, the violet kunzea grows to around 2.5 metres. The leaves are small in comparison to the flowers. In full flower this shrub makes a very attractive display as the flowers appear in profusion along the smaller branches, almost covering the whole shrub. The fluffy blossoms are mauve to purple in colour and open in the spring. Rocky elevated heath areas and open forests along the whole eastern side of Australia are its preferred sites. It is also an attractive home garden plant.

The word *parvifolia* refers to the small leaves.

Papers

Blossoms Optic Juni Purple (medium purple)
   Canson 475 Vert pomme (medium green) for flower cups
   Optic Raza Red (bright red) for stigma
Buds Canson 475 Vert pomme (medium green)
Spent blossoms Canson 475 Vert pomme (medium green) for cups
   Optic Raza Red (bright red) for stigma
Leaves Canson 475 Vert pomme (medium green)
Stems Canson 133 Sepia (medium brown)
and Scribblers SC224 Iridescent Gold dimensional paint

Construction

Blossoms
From purple paper, cut 85 strips 1 cm × 1.5 cm, finely fringed.

Stigma In bright red cut 17 strips 1.5 cm long, finely tapered.

Cups In medium green cut 17 strips 1.5 mm × 12 cm.

Attach stigma to one end of the cup strip at right angles. Coil from stigma end into a cup shape with stigma pointing up through the centre of cup:

Each blossom has 5 fringed pieces per cup. Coil each fringed piece into a tight coil. Position one piece at a time in a circle inside the cup, making sure the stigma remains centred and sticks out above fringing. When blossom is dry, spread the fringing outwards to give the blossoms a fluffy effect and brush the tips with Iridescent Gold dimensional paint.

Buds
In medium green paper, cut 3 strips 1.5 mm × 12 cm.

In purple paper, cut 3 strips 1.5 mm × 11 cm.

Coil all 6 strips into a cup shape. Fit the open end of purple cup inside the open end of the green cup, glue and dry.

From medium green paper, cut 12 small equilateral triangles with 5 mm sides. Attach 4 triangles evenly around the inside edge of each cup so they partly cover the purple centre. When dry, bend the top of each triangle slightly outwards.

Spent blossoms
Make 4 blossom cups as before, including stigma.

Leaves
From medium green paper, cut:
   41 leaves from pattern 1:
   35 leaves from pattern 2:

Emboss mid-rib from tip to base and curve the tip backwards from about halfway.

Stems

From medium brown paper, cut:

    1 strip 3 mm × 9 cm
    1 strip 3 mm × 8.5 cm
    1 strip 3 mm × 7 cm
    1 strip 3 mm × 6 cm
    2 strips 3 mm × 5 cm
    4 strips 3 mm × 4 cm
    1 strip 3 mm × 2.5 cm

Approx: 1.5 mm = ¹⁄₁₆"; 3 mm = ⅛"; 1 cm = ⅜"; 1.5 cm = ½"; 2.5 cm = 1"; 4 cm = 1½"; 5 cm = 2"; 6 cm = 2¼"; 7 cm = 2¾"; 8.5 cm = 3¼"; 9 cm = 3½"; 11 cm = 4¼"; 12 cm = 5"

Mounting

1. Position and glue stems following stem chart.
2. Position buds near the top of the tallest stems, leaving room above the buds for some leaves.
3. Position spent blossoms on the lower parts of the stems.
4. Position full blossoms singly or in groups of 2 or 3 randomly down the rest of the stems.
5. Position smaller leaves in pairs at the tips of the stems and then alternating down the upper stems, about 1 cm apart.
6. Position the larger leaves in the same alternating manner until all the leaves are used up.

Stem chart

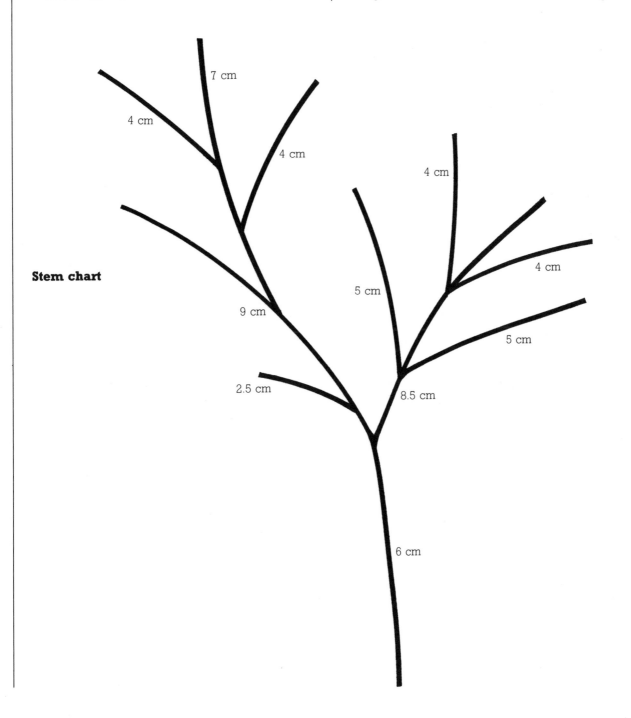

Flax wattle

Acacia linifolia

Illustrated on page 33

A spreading, graceful shrub up to 3 metres tall, with fine narrow leaves and masses of light yellow fluffy flower balls. It flowers profusely from late summer through into winter and will happily grow in almost any type of soil on the coast or tablelands along the eastern side of Australia. It creates a pleasant splash of colour during the cooler months.

The word *linifolia* refers to its narrow leaves.

Papers

Blossoms Optic Suni Yellow (pale yellow)
Leaves Canson 575 Vert billard (bright dark green)
Stems Canson 133 Sepia (brown)

Construction

Blossoms
All blossoms are cut from the yellow paper.

Large 22 strips 8 mm × 15 cm, fringed
Medium 28 strips 5 mm × 9.5 cm, fringed
Small 17 strips 3 mm × 8 cm, fringed
Buds 10 strips 3 mm × 8 cm, not fringed

Coil each strip in a tight coil. Glue and dry. Spread the fringing out and down, forming an umbrella shape around the base.

Leaves
Cut 60 leaves from the green paper from pattern 1, and 27 leaves from pattern 2:

Stems
In brown paper, cut:
   1 strip 3 mm × 19 cm
   1 strip 3 mm × 15 cm
   9 strips 1.5 mm × 3 cm
   10 strips 1.5 mm × 2 cm

Mounting

1. Position and glue stems following stem chart.
2. Position buds at the very tips of the 2 main stems in one group of 5 and one group of 3. Leave room under the group of 3 to add 2 small blossoms. Attach 1 bud at the tips of the first 2 small stems.
3. Position small blossoms, using the photograph as a guide. Add the 2 small blossoms below the 3-bud group. Place a group of 5 small blossoms below the bud on the 3 cm small stem, and a group of 4 below the other bud on the 2 cm small stem. Add a group of 4 and a group of 5 on the first 2 small stems of the other main stem.
4. Position all medium blossoms in groups of 3 or 4 on small stems below the small blossom stems. Position some blossoms at an angle.
5. Attach all large blossoms in groups of 2 or 3 to the rest of the small stems. Position some blossoms at an angle.
6. Position 6 small leaves at the tip of each of the 2 main stems, fanning them out from the tip. Add a seventh leaf, attaching it to the flat surface of the main stem so that it sticks up at an angle.
7. Position the rest of the small leaves in groups of 2 and 3 at the tips of some of the upper small stems until the small leaves are used up.
8. Position the larger leaves in an alternating pattern down the main stems, with some at the tips of the lower small stems, until all leaves are used.

Approx: 1.5 mm = $^1/_{16}$"; 3 mm = $^1/_8$"; 5 mm = $^1/_4$"; 8 mm = $^3/_8$"; 2 cm = $^3/_4$"; 3 cm = $1^1/_4$"; 8 cm = 3"; 9.5 cm = $3^3/_4$"; 15 cm = $5^3/_4$"; 19 cm = $7^3/_4$"

Stem chart

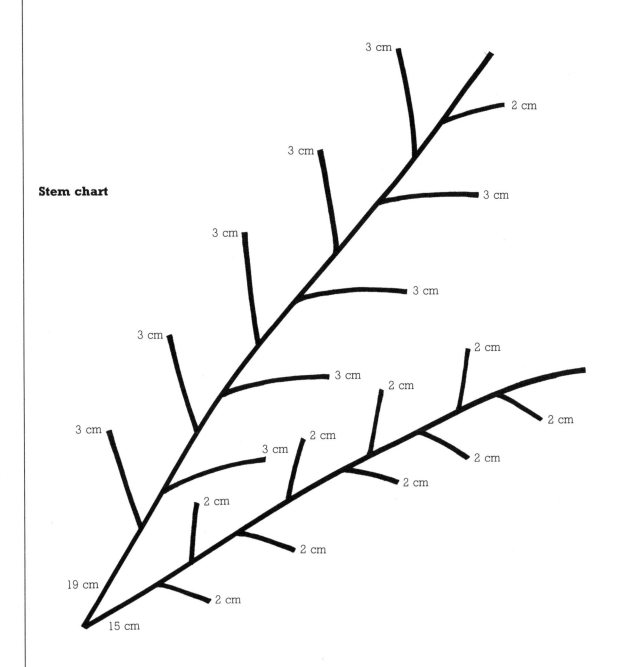

Brown boronia

(or Sweet-scented Boronia)

Boronia megastigma

Illustrated on page 43

A very dainty attractive small shrub to about 1 metre. The flowers are bi-coloured: brown on the outside and yellow inside. The cup-shaped blossoms hang downwards, either singly or in pairs. It is a very popular garden plant and suitable also as a cut flower. There are now a number of new varieties available from nurseries. Sandy soil suits the boronia best, either on the coast or the mountains, from the east coast area to the south-west of Western Australia.

The word *megastigma* refers to the large stigma.

Papers

Blossoms Optic Tera Yellow (bright yellow)
   Canson 503 Lie de vin (dark maroon brown)
Leaves Canson 475 Vert pomme (medium green)
Stems Canson 503 Lie de vin (dark maroon brown)

Construction

Open blossoms

Petals From both the yellow and dark maroon brown papers, cut a piece 5 cm × 28 cm. Glue the two pieces together and allow to dry flat under slight pressure (e.g. a heavy book). When dry cut 56 petals (4 for each blossom) from the pattern:

Curve each petal by placing it, yellow side up, on top of a soft eraser and, with a blunt round-ended instrument (such as the handle of a stitch ripper), press into the petal, pushing from the base of the petal to its tip. This makes the petal curl upwards. Bend up the square end of petal (yellow side up) at 90°

Flower centres From the dark maroon brown paper, cut 14 strips 1.5 mm × 14 cm. Coil each to a *loose* coil and glue down end before squeezing into a star shape:

Take a lump of Blu-Tack and roll into a 5 cm sausage, pressing one end down on a flat surface to anchor it firmly, and flattening the other end slightly. Gently press a star shape, flat surface down, onto the free end of the Blu-Tack. Apply some glue to the upper flat surface of the star and attach the square end of a petal, yellow side down, to it so the petal covers one point of the star. Add the next 3 petals in the same way, overlapping the square ends across the star centre. Allow to dry but do not remove from the Blu-Tack.

Calyx From green paper, cut 14 strips 1.5 mm × 7 cm. Coil them to a long cone shape, glueing inside to hold shape. When dry attach the open end of a cone to the overlapping square ends of petals on the star. When dry remove the blossom carefully from the Blu-Tack. Make 13 more blossoms the same way.

Unopened blossoms

From dark maroon brown paper only, cut 12 petals from the pattern.

Cut 3 strips 1.5 mm × 7 cm from both the dark maroon brown and green papers.

Coil each maroon strip to a tight coil. Do *not* curve these petals, but fold down centre of petal lengthwise. Bend square end of petals at 90° and attach (as for blossoms) over round coil, allowing petals to overlap each other. Coil green strips to a cone shape (as for blossoms) and attach in the same way.

Leaves

From the green paper, cut 28 leaves from pattern 1 and 24 leaves from pattern 2.

Emboss mid-rib from tip to base.

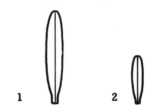

Approx: 1.5 mm = ¹⁄₁₆"; 3 mm = ⅛"; 1.5 cm = ½"; 5 cm = 2"; 6 cm = 2¼"; 7 cm = 2¾"; 10 cm = 4"; 13 cm = 5¼"; 14 cm = 5½"; 16 cm = 6¼"; 28 cm = 11"

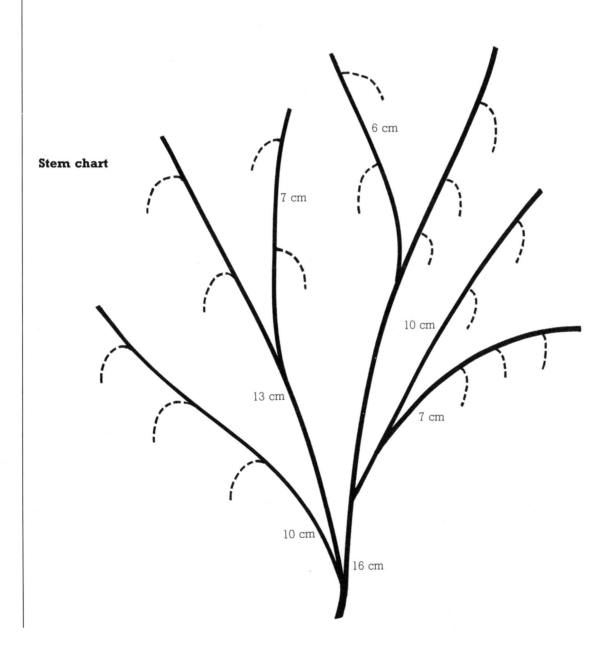

Stem chart

Main stems

From the dark maroon brown paper, cut:

    1 strip 3 mm × 16 cm
    1 strip 3 mm × 13 cm
    2 strips 3 mm × 10 cm
    2 strips 3 mm × 7 cm
    1 strip 3 mm × 6 cm

Flower stems

In dark maroon brown paper, cut 17 strips 1.5 mm × 1.5 cm.

Mounting

1. Position and glue main stems following stem chart.
2. Position flower stems, curving each strip and attaching a single stem to each of the main stems about 1 cm down from the tip. Fix the flower stems so they curve up and then hang downwards, following the dotted lines and the photograph.
3. Space the rest of the flower stems about 3 cm apart on 6 of the 7 main stems. Most should be on the same side of the stem, although you can alternate them on the 2 shorter stems.
4. On the 7th main stem attach the flower stems about 1.5 cm apart (for the unopened blossoms).
5. Attach unopened blossoms by the green calyx as shown in the photograph—make sure they hang downwards.
6. Attach all open blossoms to the flower stems by the green calyx, positioning them all to hang downwards.
7. Attach the smaller leaves, pointing upwards in groups of 2 or 3 at the tips of the main stems and opposite the first flower stems.
8. Attach the larger leaves, pointing upwards in groups of 2 or 3, opposite the other flower stems.

Brown boronia *(instructions page 40)*

Cream grevillea *(instructions page 56)*

Grevillea 'Poorinda Royal Mantle' *(instructions page 59)*

Spiky wattle

Spiky wattle

Acacia oxycedrus

A straggly, stiff and open shrub that grows to about 3 metres. The leaves are rather stiff too, with sharply pointed ends, making the plant prickly to touch. The prominent flower heads are rod-shaped, up to 20 cm long in some cases, and are bright golden yellow. Flowering starts in the spring and can continue well into winter. Well drained light to medium soils suit this shrub. It is found naturally along the eastern side of Australia from the coast and into the mountains.

The word *oxycedrus* means 'sharp-pointed'.

Papers

Blossoms   Optic Tera Yellow (bright yellow)
Leaves   Canson 448 Vert ocean (very dark green)
Stems   Canson 448 Vert ocean (very dark green)

Construction

Blossoms
From the yellow paper, cut 168 strips 7 mm × 5 cm, finely fringed (14 pieces for each blossom).

Coil each piece into a tight coil and glue together in rows of 7, being careful not to glue the fringing.

Allow to dry thoroughly, then glue 2 strips of 7 side-by-side into pairs, again avoiding the fringing. Allow to dry, then spread the fringing outwards.

Half-open blossom
From the yellow paper, cut 6 strips 7 mm × 5 cm, finely fringed, coil tightly, glue into 2 rows of 3 then join together in parallel, again avoiding fringing.

From the yellow paper, cut 8 strips 5 mm × 5 cm, coil tightly and join into 2 rows of 4. When dry glue the 2 rows together, and glue the fringed pieces to one end to form a full length blossom.

Buds
From the yellow paper, cut 14 strips 5 mm × 5 cm, coil tightly and join together (2 rows of 7) as for full blossom.

Flower stems
From the yellow paper, cut 11 strips 5 mm × 1 cm long. Roll them into a small tube and glue, using a fine knitting needle or something similar to form them. Attach them to 11 of the main flower heads.

From the yellow paper, cut 3 strips 3 mm × 1 cm, roll into small tubes and glue. Attach these 3 mm rolls to one end of the bud group, the half-open blossom and the remaining full blossom.

Leaves
From the dark green paper, cut:
   40 leaves from pattern 1:
   62 leaves from pattern 2:
   20 leaves from pattern 3:
Emboss mid-rib from base to tip.

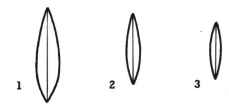

Stems
From dark green paper, cut:
   2 strips 3 mm × 19 cm
   1 strip 3 mm × 16 cm

48 | ## Mounting

1. Position and glue stems following stem chart.
2. Position the bud group at the tip of one stem.
3. Position half-open flower head at the tip of another stem.
4. Position 1 full flower head at the tip of the third stem.
5. Position the rest of the blossoms at 30° to the stem at points 3–6 cm apart, following the photograph—5 blossoms on one stem and 3 blossoms on the other two stems.
6. Attach leaves, using smallest first, alternating them down the top sections of all stems. Attach some of the leaves to the flat surface of the main stem so they stand up above the stem for an extra 3-dimensional effect.
7. Attach the medium leaves next in the same way.
8. Attach the largest leaves in the same way on the bottom sections of the stems.

Stem chart

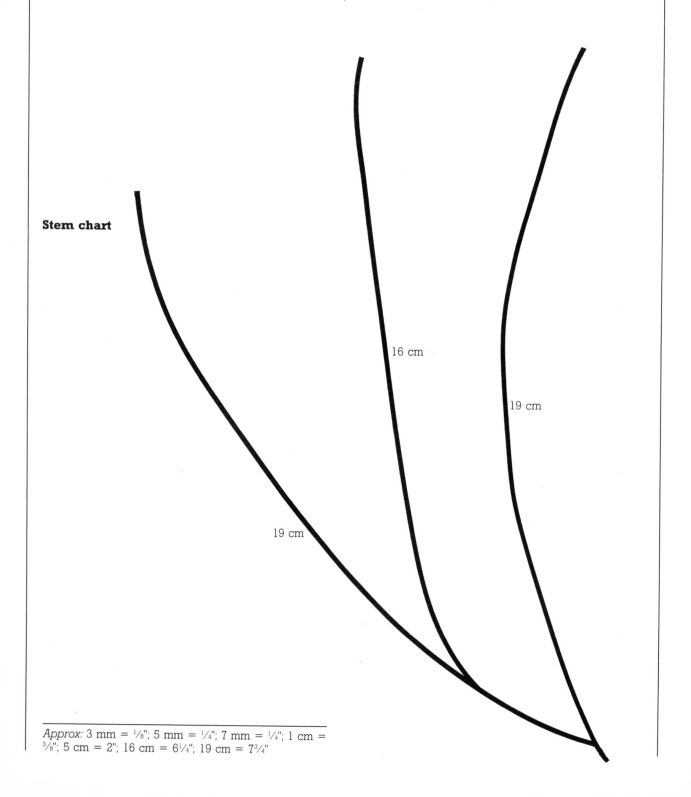

16 cm

19 cm

19 cm

Approx: 3 mm = ⅛"; 5 mm = ¼"; 7 mm = ¼"; 1 cm = ⅜"; 5 cm = 2"; 16 cm = 6¼"; 19 cm = 7¾"

Mottlecah

Eucalyptus macrocarpa

Illustrated on page 34

A rather straggly small shrub that grows to about 2 metres. The stem-clasping silver grey leaves make an attractive background for the huge 10 cm red, sometimes pink or yellowish, flowers. The plant has a number of common names, including Mallee Rose, Rose of the West and Desert Pride. It flowers throughout most of the year but is at its best in winter and spring. The bark is grey or light brown. The woody flower cups are silver grey like the leaves. The Mottlecah grows naturally in open sandy heath areas in south-western Western Australia.

The word *macrocarpa* refers to the large fruit.

Papers

Blossoms and buds Optic Raza Red (bright red)
  Optic Copa Green (light green) for centre
  Optic Suni Yellow (yellow) for stigma
Base cups Optic Zena Grey (light grey)
Old blossoms Optic Zena Grey (light grey)
  Optic Koda Caramel (light orange)
  Optic Vada Blonde (cream)
Leaves Optic Zena Grey (light grey)
Stems Optic Zena Grey (light grey) double thickness
and Scribblers SC224 Iridescent Gold dimensional paint

Construction

Blossoms
In red, cut 15 strips 1 cm × 21 cm, finely fringed.

Centres Cut 15 strips 2 mm × 21 cm in pale green.

Stigmas Cut 15 tapered 1 cm long strips in yellow.

Join 1 fringed strip to the end of 1 green strip and attach the stigma at right angles to the other end of the green strip. The fringing and stigma must both be facing the same direction. Coil flat from stigma end—do *not* form a cup.

Base cups From grey paper, cut 8 strips 2 mm × 60 cm and coil to a deep wide cup to fit the base of the blossom. Coat inside cup with glue to hold shape, allow to dry, then fit blossom base inside cup. The remaining 7 blossoms without cups are attached flat when mounting. Brush the fringed tips of all the flowers with Iridescent Gold dimensional paint.

Half-open bud with cap
Cut 1 strip 1 cm × 11.5 cm from red paper, finely fringed. Cut 1 strip 2 mm × 45 cm from grey paper. Measure 7.5 cm in from one end of grey strip and glue the uncut edge of the red fringed strip to the grey strip (to 19 cm). Allow to dry, then coil from the long grey end into a cup shape until you reach the fringed section, coiling straight until you are past the fringing. Apply glue to the last section of grey strip before continuing to coil straight (this will hold the top section firm).

For the cap cut 1 strip 2 mm × 40 cm in grey and coil to a wide cup shape with a pointed tip.

Coat inside with glue. When dry fit at an angle over most of the fringing as in the photograph. The exposed fringing can be spread out slightly and the tips brushed with Iridescent Gold dimensional paint.

50

Unopened bud

Cut 2 strips 2 mm × 40 cm in grey. Coil one to a pointed cup (as for the cap for the half-opened bud). Coil the other strip to cup with a less pointed end. Coat inside both cups with glue, allow to dry. Glue the open ends together. The more pointed end is the cap of the bud.

Old blossoms

Cut:

1 strip 2 mm × 40 cm in grey
3 strips 2 mm × 12.5 cm in light green
3 strips 2 mm × 12.5 cm in orange
3 strips 2 mm × 12.5 cm in cream
3 long tapered 1 cm strips in yellow for the stigmas

Centre Join into one long strip one strip each of cream, then light green and orange. Attach the stigma to the free end of the cream strip at right angles. Coil from stigma end into a tight coil. Coil the 40 cm grey strip into a tight coil and glue to the bottom of the cream, green and orange coil, making sure the stigma is on top.

Cups Cut 2 strips 2 mm × 45 cm in grey paper and coil to a wide cup. Glue the centre flat inside the cup, keeping the stigma to the top.

Approx: 2 mm = $^{3}/_{32}$"; 1 cm = $^{3}/_{8}$"; 5 cm = 2"; 7 cm = $2^{3}/_{4}$"; 7.5 cm = $2^{7}/_{8}$"; 9.5 cm = $3^{3}/_{4}$"; 11.5 cm = $4^{1}/_{2}$"; 12.5 cm = 5"; 19 cm = $7^{1}/_{2}$"; 21 cm = $8^{1}/_{4}$"; 40 cm = 16"; 45 cm = 18"

Stem chart

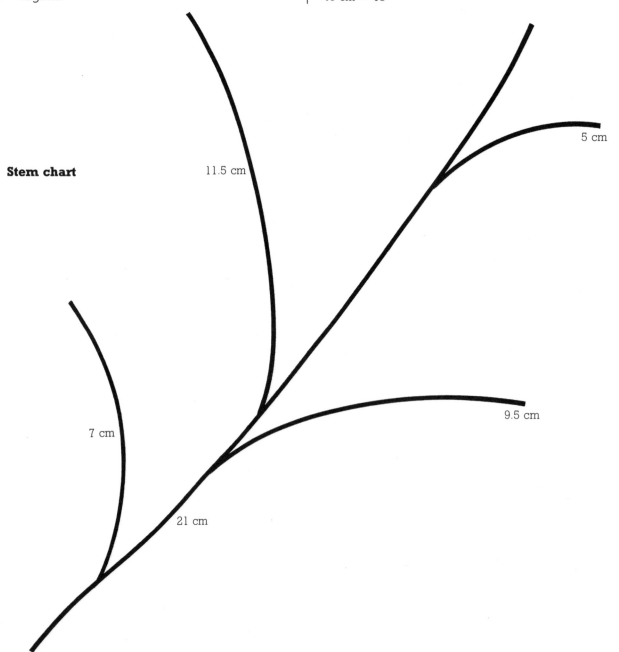

11.5 cm

5 cm

9.5 cm

7 cm

21 cm

Leaves

In grey paper, cut:

    43 leaves from pattern 1:

    21 leaves from pattern 2:

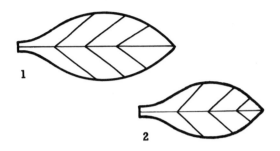

Emboss mid-rib and side veins; using a fine blade draw each leaf over the blade (like curling ribbon), to curve it slightly.

Stems

From the grey paper, cut:

    2 strips 3 mm × 21 cm

    2 strips 3 mm × 11.5 cm

    2 strips 3 mm × 9.5 cm

    2 strips 3 mm × 7 cm

    2 strips 3 mm × 5 cm

and glue each pair of strips together.

Mounting

1. Position and glue stems following stem chart.
2. Attach a blossom to the tip of the 11.5 cm stem.
3. Attach the bud to the tip of the 21 cm stem.
4. Attach an old blossom to the tip of the 7 cm stem. Attach one of the other old blossoms 1 cm below the first, placing the last one 1 cm below the second one but on the other side of the stem.
5. Following the photograph, attach all the blossoms alternately down the stems at 1 cm spacing, placing those with cups at an angle and those without cups flat.
6. All the leaves curve upwards and curve around and over the stems and blossoms. The side leaves are attached to the flat surface of the stem, while the top covering leaves are attached to the top edge of the stem by folding the base of the leaf over the stem and glueing.
7. Attach the smaller leaves, one at the tips of each of 2 stems, and the rest alternating down all stems.
8. Attach the larger leaves in the same way at 1–2 cm spacing until all are used up.

Blue berry ash

Elaeocarpus reticulatus

Illustrated on page 55

A small, attractive tree that grows to 10 metres or more. It makes a good street, park or garden tree. The finely fringed bell-shaped flowers, usually white but sometimes pink, give the tree a fairy-like appearance. The bark is brown, either smooth or wrinkled. The young leaves are often pink, turning light green, then dark green and eventually red when fully mature. The fruits that follow the flowers are bright blue berries (hence the common name). The fruit is a favourite food for many native birds. Flowers appear mainly in the winter. The tree grows in sub-tropical areas, along river flats, in the gullies and rainforests of the Northern Territory, Queensland and northern New South Wales.

The word *elaeocarpus* means 'olive fruit', and *reticulatus* refers to the network of veins on the leaves.

Papers

Blossoms   Optic Vada Blonde (cream)
Stigma   Optic Vada Blonde (cream)
Buds   Optic Vada Blonde (cream)
Spent blossoms   Optic Vada Blonde (cream)
   Canson 130 Terre rouge (rust red)
   Canson 475 Vert pomme (medium green)
Leaves   Canson 130 Terre rouge (rust red)
   Canson 475 Vert pomme (medium green)
Main stems   Canson 448 Vert ocean (ivy green)
Small stems   Canson 130 Terre rouge (rust red)

Construction

Blossoms
From the cream paper, cut:
   40 strips 5 mm × 23 mm, fringed
   40 strips 2 mm ×22 cm, plain

Stigma Cut 40 thin tapered strips 8 mm long in cream paper.

Join one end of fringed strip to one end of plain strip, attaching stigma at right angles to the other end of the plain strip. Coil from stigma end, forming a cup shape with a slightly flattened top with the stigma inside the cup. Apply glue to the base of the fringed strip *before* coiling the fringed section.

Buds
From the cream paper, cut:
   13 strips 2 mm × 7 cm
   13 strips 2 mm × 6 cm

Coil the 7 cm strip into a cone shape:

Coil the 6 cm strip into a cup shape:

Glue the open ends together.

Spent blossoms
Cut 3 strips 2 mm × 6 cm from the rust red paper.
Cut 3 strips 2 mm × 6 cm in medium green paper.
Cut 3 stigmas in cream paper.

Coil rust red into a cup shape. Attach stigma at right angles to one end of the green strip and coil from stigma end into a shallow cup. Join open end of rust cup to the open end of the green cup with the stigma protruding.

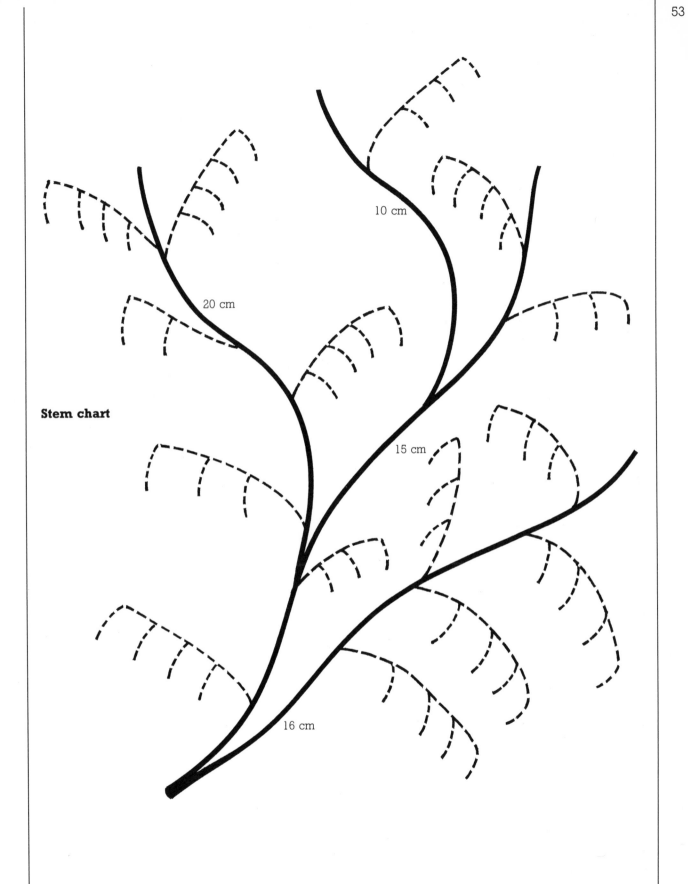

Stem chart

10 cm

20 cm

15 cm

16 cm

Leaves

Cut 24 leaves in green from pattern 1.
Cut 7 leaves in green and 3 leaves in rust from pattern 2.
Cut 4 leaves in rust from pattern 3.
Cut 5 leaves from pattern 4.

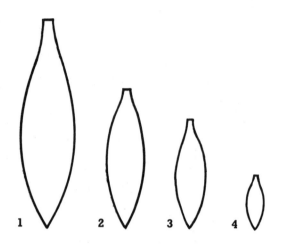

Emboss mid-rib and side veins following the patterns below. Cut small triangles along side veins to create a notched leaf edge. Fold pattern 1 leaves down the mid-rib—open out but do not straighten.

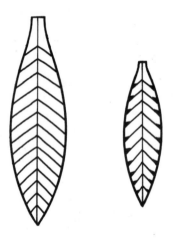

Approx: 2 mm = ³/₃₂"; 5 mm = ¼"; 8 mm = ³/₈"; 1 cm = ³/₈"; 4 cm = 1½"; 5 cm = 2"; 6 cm = 2¼"; 7 cm = 2³/₄"; 10 cm = 4"; 15 cm = 6"; 16 cm = 6¼"; 20 cm = 8"

Main stems

From the ivy green paper, cut:
1 strip 3 mm × 20 cm
1 strip 3 mm × 16 cm
1 strip 3 mm × 15 cm
1 strip 3 mm × 10 cm

Minor stems

From the rust red paper, cut:
11 strips 2 mm × 5 cm
5 strips 2 mm × 4 cm

Curve one end of each strip where it will be attached to a main stem.

Blossom stems

In rust red paper, cut 56 strips 2 mm × 1 cm. Curve each strip slightly.

Mounting

1. Position and glue main stems following the stem chart.
2. Attach minor stems and blossom stems following the broken lines on the stem chart.
3. All blossoms, buds and spent blossoms hang downwards from their stems, with only one to a stem.
4. Following the photograph, attach buds to some of the outer blossom stems.
5. Attach spent blossoms to some of the lower blossom stems, as in the photograph.
6. Attach a single blossom to the remaining stems, positioning some at a slight angle. Spread the fringing a little on some flowers while leaving others straight.
7. Following the photograph, attach the smallest rust leaves as 2 pairs and a single to the very tips of 3 of the main stems.
8. Attach the larger rust leaves at the tips of the main stems behind the small rust leaves.
9. Attach the medium green leaves alternately down the main stems in the upper section.
10. Attach the largest green leaves to the remaining main stems in an alternating pattern, about 3 cm apart, right to the bottom of the stems.

Blue berry ash *(instructions page 52)*

Cream grevillea

Grevillea australis

Illustrated on page 44

A stiff, rambling, low-growing shrub very variable in height and width which can be prostrate or upright. The cream or white flowers are almost stalkless and appear in late spring and into summer. It makes a dense ground cover. Preferring the cooler sub-alpine areas of Tasmania and Victoria, where it likes a medium soil in protected pockets, it will adapt to a variety of other areas below the sub-tropical zones.

The word *australis* means 'southern'.

Papers

Blossoms Optic Vada Blonde (cream)
   Canson 475 Vert pomme (mid green)
Leaves Canson 480 Vert amande (pale green)
   Canson 475 Vert pomme (medium green)
   Canson 448 Vert ocean (dark ivy green)
Leaf stems Canson 130 Terre rouge (rust red)
Main stems Canson 501 Marron fonce (maroon brown)
and Scribblers SC136 Shiny Chiffon Green dimensional paint

Construction

Blossoms
From the cream paper, cut 28 rectangles 5 mm × 5 cm. Mark a line across the rectangle 1 cm in from one end. Mark the remainder of the strip into 3 equal widths and cut along the marked lines to 1 cm mark—do not cut through the 1 cm section.

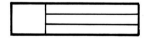

Fold the 1 cm section along continuations of the 3 lines, fold concertina-fashion and glue.

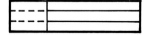

Coil the long strips one at a time into a loose coil, coiling all in the same direction.

Stigmas Cut 84 small strips 1 mm × 1 cm in cream paper. Attach 1 small strip to the back of each loose coil so it protrudes past the coiled section:

When glue has dried dip the tips of the stigmas in Shiny Chiffon Green dimensional paint.

Base cup In mid green paper, cut 28 strips 1.5 mm × 3 cm. Coil into a small cup shape, press slightly sideways and fit and glue over the folded end of the blossom.

Leaves
Cut 15 leaves from pattern 1 in pale green.
Cut 28 leaves from pattern 2 in medium green and 11 leaves in dark green.

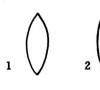

1   2

Stem chart

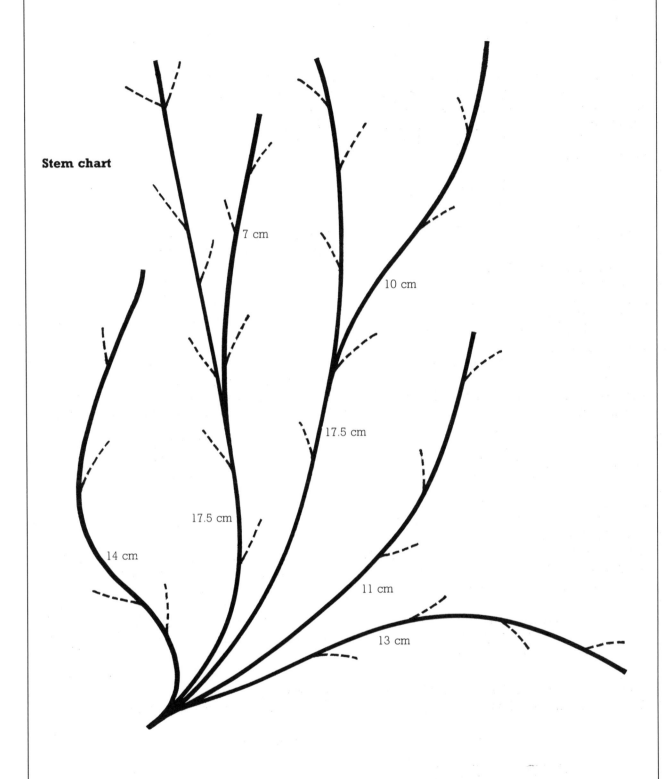

7 cm

10 cm

17.5 cm

17.5 cm

14 cm

11 cm

13 cm

58   Cut 45 leaves from pattern 3 in medium green and 8 leaves in dark green:

3

Emboss mid-rib on each leaf. Also emboss the sides of each leaf, for the full length of the leaf, following the curve 1–2 mm in from the edge.

Leaf stems
Cut 29 strips 1.5 mm × 1 cm in rust red paper.

Main stems
In dark brown paper cut:
   2 strips 2 mm × 17.5 cm
   1 strip 2 mm × 14 cm
   1 strip 2 mm × 13 cm
   1 strip 2 mm × 11 cm
   1 strip 2 mm × 10 cm
   1 strip 2 mm × 7 cm

Mounting

1. Position and glue main stems following the stem chart.
2. Attach leaf stems in positions indicated by broken lines.
3. All leaves point toward the tips of the leaf stems.
4. Attach pairs or threes of the small leaves to the tips of the main stems (pale and medium green). Use the photograph as a guide.
5. Attach the middle-sized leaves in groups of 3 to the tips of the leaf stems on the upper sections of the main stems in colour groups of your choice.
6. Attach the large leaves, in any colour combination you like, in groups of 3 on the leaf stems down the lower main stems.
7. Using the photograph as a guide, attach the blossoms by the green cup *only* to the main stems just below the leaf stems and on the same side. The blossoms overlay the leaves.

Approx: 1 mm = $\frac{3}{64}$"; 1.5 mm = $\frac{1}{16}$"; 2 mm = $\frac{3}{32}$"; 5 mm = $\frac{1}{4}$"; 1 cm = $\frac{3}{8}$"; 3 cm = $1\frac{1}{4}$"; 5 cm = 2"; 7 cm = $2\frac{3}{4}$"; 10 cm = 4"; 11 cm = $4\frac{1}{4}$"; 13 cm = $5\frac{1}{4}$"; 14 cm = $5\frac{1}{2}$"; 17.5 cm = $6\frac{3}{4}$"

Grevillea 'Poorinda Royal Mantle'

Grevillea laurifolia × willisi

Illustrated on page 45

A popular hybrid grevillea developed by Leo Hodge in his garden at Bairnsdale, Victoria. This attractive vigorous groundcover spreads to about 3 metres. It is a rather stiff plant and covers a large area with strong red toothbrush-type flowers in marked contrast to the leaves which are dark green on the top surface and silver-green-grey on the underside. It is a profuse flowerer and hardy even in colder climates, coping with some frosts. Its ability to cope even with heavy soils, from coast to mountain areas, makes it a popular garden plant throughout most of Australia. 'Poorinda Royal Mantle' is not found naturally in the wild.

Papers

Blossoms   Optic Coro Crimson (red)
Leaves   Canson 448 Vert ocean (dark green) for upper surface
   Optic Copa Green (light green) for underside
Stems   Canson 501 Marron fonce (maroon brown)
and Scribblers SC203 Golden Yellow dimensional paint

Construction

Blossoms
Cut from red paper, following diagrams carefully as this is a complicated construction.

Cut 1 blossom outline from pattern 1.
Cut 1 blossom outline from pattern 2.
Cut 8 blossom outlines from pattern 3.

With a soft pencil draw a line 1 cm in from the small end. Draw a line 1 mm in from the wide end. (When cutting the strips you must not cut through either of these sections.) Mark a centre line down the full length of each piece—this is a guide for the cutting of the strips. Draw lines parallel with the outside edges, 1 mm in from the edge, from the 1 cm line at one end to the 1 mm line at the other end. Now draw in the lines on the diagram.

Using a *very* sharp blade cut through the solid lines, taking great care not to cut too far. Cut away the small triangle section from the wide end (indicated by solid black patch). Now cut away the 1 mm section at the wide end to free one end of the strips.

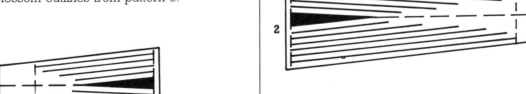

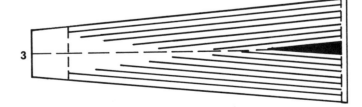

60

Coil the outside strip on both sides in the same direction into a loose coil. Coil all the other strips into loose coils, one at a time, in the *opposite* direction to the outside coils. Fold the sides of the 1 cm end in over the middle (see diagram) to bring the 2 outside coils over to the same side as the other coils. Glue the folds in place.

fold the sides in over the middle

Stigmas Cut a strip 1 mm × 1 cm in red for *each* coil (but as the coils get smaller reduce the length a little). Attach a stigma strip to the back of each coil:

Dip the tip of each stigma in Golden Yellow dimensional paint.

Cups In dark green paper, cut 10 strips 2 mm × 10 cm. Coil into a small cup and attach over the folded end of each blossom.

Leaves

For *large leaves*, cut 2 pieces of dark green paper 18 cm × 35 cm, and 2 pieces of light green paper the same size. Glue dark green sheets to light green sheets and dry under light pressure to keep flat. Cut 8 leaves from pattern 1.

For *medium leaves*, cut 2 pieces of dark green paper 16 cm × 28 cm, and 2 pieces of light green paper the same size. Glue together, light and dark, as for the large leaf, and cut 7 leaves from pattern 2.

For *small leaves*, cut 2 pieces dark green paper and 2 pieces light green paper 18 cm × 23 cm. Glue together, dark and light, and cut 9 leaves from pattern 3.

Emboss each leaf on the dark green side with a mid-rib and side veins from the tip of each leaf lobe to the mid-rib. Fold and crease each leaf down the mid-rib, open out but do not straighten. Slightly twist some of the lobes of the largest leaves to show the light green underside.

Stems

In brown paper, cut:
  1 strip 3 mm × 22 cm
  2 strips 3 mm × 18 cm
  1 strip 3 mm × 10.5 cm
  2 strips 3 mm × 9.5 cm
  1 strip 3 mm × 7 cm

Approx: 1 mm = ³⁄₆₄"; 2 mm = ³⁄₃₂"; 3 mm = ³⁄₁₆"; 1 cm = ³⁄₈"; 7 cm = 2³⁄₄"; 9.5 cm = 3³⁄₄"; 10 cm = 4"; 10.5 cm = 4¹⁄₄"; 16 cm = 6¹⁄₄"; 18 cm = 7"; 22 cm = 8³⁄₄"; 28 cm = 11"; 35 cm = 13³⁄₄"

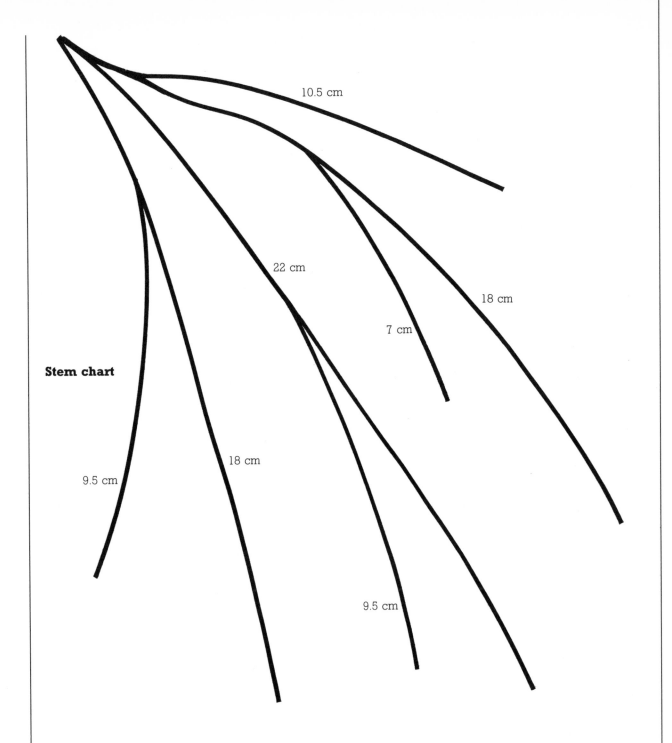

Stem chart

10.5 cm

22 cm

18 cm

7 cm

18 cm

9.5 cm

9.5 cm

Mounting

1. Attach stems following the stem chart.

2. All leaves are attached to the stems at an acute angle, pointing toward the stem tips.

3. Attach 1 small leaf to the tip of each stem.

4. Using the photograph as a guide, attach the rest of the leaves in alternating pattern, with small leaves near the tips of the stems, the medium leaves next and the large leaves near the base of the stems. The leaves will be very crowded and overlap, but this is true to the plant's style of growth.

5. Attach the 2 smaller blossoms near the tips of 2 of the stems, just below a small leaf. The blossom should lie in the crease of the leaf.

6. Attach the rest of the blossoms randomly along the stems, pointing in the same direction as the leaves.

Reading list

Other titles on Quilling from Kangaroo Press:
- *The Art of Quilling*, Trees Tra & Pieter Van De Wolk, 1993
- *Creative Quilling*, Trees Tra & Pieter Van De Wolk, 1994
- *Decorative Quilling*, Trees Tra & Malinda Johnston, 1993

Readers may also be interested in working out their own floral designs. I found Leonard Cronin's book very helpful in this regard:
- *The Concise Australian Flora*, Leonard Cronin, Reed Books Pty Ltd, 1989

Index